THE GOLDEN TOUCH

NIGHT LIGHTS

THE GOLDEN TOUCH

ILLUSTRATED BY

RICHARD SALVUCCI

NIGHT LIGHTS

NATHANIEL HAWTHORNE

St. Martin's Press/New York

Published by St. Martin's Press
175 Fifth Avenue, New York, New York 10010.

The NIGHT LIGHTS series is produced by Armadillo Press.

Library of Congress Cataloging-in-Publication Data

Hawthorne, Nathaniel, 1804-1864.
The golden touch.

(Night light series)
        Summary: King Midas's fondest wish,
to have everything he touches turn to gold, backfires.
        1. Midas—Juvenile literature. [1. Midas.
2. Mythology, Greek] I. Title. II. Series.
BL820.M55H38 1986 398.2'2 [E] 86-31629
ISBN 0-312-57284-0

Book design and original NIGHT LIGHTS concept by:
Dave Orlon
Production: Richard Salvucci

Typesetting: Robert K. Wiener/ARCHITYPE
Special thanks to Carol and Steven, Parkinson International.

Manufactured in South Korea

THE GOLDEN TOUCH

NIGHT LIGHTS

Once upon a time, there lived a very rich man, and a king besides, whose name was Midas; and he had a little daughter, whom nobody but myself ever heard of, and whose name I either never knew, or have entirely forgotten. So, because I love odd names for little girls, I choose to call her Marygold.

This King Midas was fonder of gold than of anything else in the world. He valued his royal crown chiefly because it was composed of that precious metal. If he loved anything better, or half so well, it was the one little maiden who played so merrily around her father's footstool. But the more Midas loved his daughter, the more did he desire and seek for wealth. He thought, foolish man! that the best thing he could possibly do for this dear child would be to bequeath her the immensest pile of yellow, glistening coin that had ever been heaped together since the world was made. Thus, he gave all his thoughts and all his time to this one purpose. If ever he happened to gaze for an instant at the gold-tinted clouds of sunset, he wished that they were real gold, and that they could be squeezed safely into his strongbox. When little Marygold ran to meet him with a bunch of buttercups and dandelions, he used to say, "Poh, poh, child! If these flowers were as golden as they look, they would be worth the plucking!"

And yet, in his earlier days, before he was so entirely possessed of this insane desire for riches, King Midas had shown a great taste for flowers. He had planted a garden, in which grew the biggest and beautifullest and sweetest roses that any mortal ever saw or smelt. These roses were still growing in the garden, as large, as lovely, and as fragrant as when Midas used to pass whole hours in gazing at them, and inhaling their perfume. But now if he looked at them at all it was only to calculate how much the garden would be worth if each of the innumerable rose petals were a thin plate of gold. And though he once was fond of music (in spite of an idle story about his ears, which were said to resemble those of an ass), the only music for poor Midas, now, was the chink of one coin against another.

At length (as people always grow more and more foolish, unless they take care to grow wiser and wiser), Midas had got to be so exceedingly unreasonable that he could scarcely bear to see or touch any object that was not gold. He made it his custom, therefore, to pass a large portion of every day in a dark and dreary apartment, underground, at the basement of his palace. It was here that he kept his wealth. To this dismal hole—for it was little better than a dungeon—Midas betook himself whenever he wanted to be particularly happy. Here, after carefully locking the door, he would take a bag of gold coin, or a gold cup as big as a washbowl, or a heavy golden bar, or a peck-measure of gold dust and bring them from the obscure corners of the room into the one bright and narrow sunbeam that fell from the dungeonlike window. He valued the sunbeam for no other reason but that his treasure would not shine without its help. And then would he reckon over the coins in the bag; toss up the bar, and catch it as it came down; sift the gold dust through his fingers; look at the funny image of his own face as reflected in the burnished circumference of the cup; and whisper to himself, "O Midas, rich King Midas, what a happy man art thou!" But it was laughable to see how the image of his face kept grinning at him out of the polished surface of the cup. It seemed to be aware of his foolish behavior, and to have a naughty inclination to make fun of him.

Midas called himself a happy man, but felt that he was not yet quite so happy as he might be. The very tip-top of enjoyment would never be reached unless the whole world were to become his treasure-room, and be filled with yellow metal, which should be all his own.

Now, I need hardly remind such wise little people as you are that in the old, old times, when King Midas was alive, a great many things came to pass that we should consider wonderful if they were to happen in our own day and country. And, on the other hand, a great many things take place nowadays that seem not only wonderful to us, but at which the people of old times would have stared their eyes out. On the whole, I regard our own times as the strangest of the two; but, however that may be, I must go on with my story.

Midas was enjoying himself in his treasure-room one day, as usual, when he perceived a shadow fall over the heaps of gold; and, looking suddenly up, what should he behold but the figure of a stranger, standing in the bright and narrow sunbeam! It was a young man, with a cheerful and ruddy face. Whether it was that the imagination of King Midas threw a yellow tinge over everything, or whatever the cause might be, he could not help fancying that the smile with which the stranger regarded him had a kind of golden radiance in it. Certainly, although his figure intercepted the sunshine, there was now a brighter gleam upon all the piled-up treasures than before. Even the remotest corners had their share of it, and were lighted up when the stranger smiled, as with tips of flame and sparkles of fire. As Midas knew that he had carefully turned the key in the lock, and that no mortal strength could possibly break into his treasure-room, he of course concluded that his visitor must be something more than mortal. It is no matter about telling you who he was. In those days, when the earth was comparatively a new affair, it was supposed to be often the resort of beings endowed with supernatural power, and who used to interest themselves in the joys and sorrows of men, women, and children, half playfully and half seriously. Midas had met such beings before now and was not sorry to meet one of them again. The stranger's aspect, indeed was so good-humored and kindly, if not beneficent, that it would have been unreasonable to suspect him of intending any mischief. It was far more probable that he came to do Midas a favor. And what could that favor be unless to multiply his heaps of treasure?

The stranger gazed about the room. And when his lustrous smile had glistened upon all the golden objects that were there, he turned again to Midas.

"You are a wealthy man, friend Midas!" he observed. "I doubt whether any other four walls on earth contain so much gold as you have contrived to pile up in this room."

"I have done pretty well—pretty well," answered Midas in a discontented tone. "But, after all, it is but a trifle when you consider that it has taken me my whole life to get it together. If one could live a thousand years, he might have time to grow rich!"

"What!" exclaimed the stranger. "Then you are not satisfied?"

Midas shook his head.

"And pray what would satisfy you?" asked the stranger. "Merely for the curiosity of the thing, I should be glad to know."

Midas paused and meditated. He felt a presentiment that this stranger, with such a golden luster in his goodhumored smile, had come hither with both the power and the purpose of gratifying his utmost wishes. Now, therefore, was the fortunate moment when he had but to speak, and obtain whatever possible, or seemingly impossible thing, it might come into his head to ask. So he thought, and thought, and thought, and heaped up one golden mountain upon another in his imagination, without being able to imagine them big enough. At last a bright idea occurred to King Midas. It seemed really as bright as the glistening metal that he loved so much.

Raising his head, he looked the lustrous stranger in the face.

"Well, Midas," observed the visitor, "I see that you have at length hit upon something that will satisfy you. Tell me your wish."

"It is only this," replied Midas. "I am weary of collecting my treasures with so much trouble, and beholding the heap so diminutive, after I have done my best. I wish everything that I touch to be changed to gold!"

The stranger's smile grew so very broad that it seemed to fill the room like an outburst of the sun gleaming into a shadowy dell where the yellow autumnal leaves—for so looked the lumps and particles of gold—lie strewn in the glow of light.

"The Golden Touch!" exclaimed he. "You certainly deserve credit, friend Midas, for striking out so brilliant a conception. But are you quite sure that this will satisfy you?"

"How could it fail?" said Midas.

"And you will never regret the possession of it?"

"What could induce me?" asked Midas. "I ask nothing else to render me perfectly happy."

"Be it as you wish, then," replied the stranger, waving his hand in token of farewell. "Tomorrow, at sunrise, you will find yourself gifted with the Golden Touch."

The figure of the stranger then became exceedingly bright, and Midas involuntarily closed his eyes. On opening them again he beheld only one yellow sunbeam in the room and all around him the glistening of the precious metal that he had spent his life hoarding up.

Whether Midas slept as usual that night, the story does not say. Asleep or awake, however, his mind was probably in the state of a child's, to whom a beautiful new plaything has been promised in the morning. At any rate, day had hardly peeped over the hills when King Midas was broad awake and, stretching his arms out of bed, began to touch objects that were within reach. He was anxious to prove whether the Golden Touch had really come, according to the stranger's promise. So he laid his finger on a chair by the bedside, and on various other things, but was grievously disappointed to perceive that they remained of exactly the same substance as before. Indeed, he felt very much afraid that he had only dreamed about the lustrous stranger, or else that the latter had been making game of him. And what a miserable affair would it be if, after all his hopes, Midas must content himself with what little gold he could scrape together by ordinary means, instead of creating it by a touch!

All this while it was only the gray of the morning, with but a streak of brightness along the edge of the sky where Midas could not see it. He lay in a very disconsolate mood, regretting the downfall of his hopes, and kept growing sadder and sadder until the earliest sunbeam shone through the window and gilded the ceiling over his head. It seemed to Midas that this bright yellow sunbeam was reflected in rather a singular way on the white covering of the bed. Looking more closely, what was his astonishment and delight when he found that this linen fabric had been transmuted to what seemed a woven texture of the purest and brightest gold! The Golden Touch had come to him with the first sunbeam!

Midas started up in a kind of joyful frenzy and ran about the room, grasping at everything that happened to be in his way. He seized one of the bedposts, and it became immediately a fluted golden pillar. He pulled aside

a windowcurtain in order to admit a clear spectacle of the wonders that he was performing; and the tassel grew heavy in his hand—a mass of gold. He took up a book from the table. At his first touch it assumed the appearance of such a splendidly bound and guilt-edged volume as one often meets with, nowadays; but, on running his fingers through the leaves, behold! it was a bundle of thin gold plates, in which all the wisdom of the book had grown illegible. He hurriedly put on his clothes and was enraptured to see himself in a magnificent suit of gold cloth, which retained its flexibility and softness, although it burdened him a little with its weight. He drew out his handkerchief, which little Marygold had hemmed for him. That was likewise gold, with the dear child's neat and pretty stitches running all along the border, in gold thread!

Somehow or other this last transformation did not quite please King Midas. He would rather that his little daughter's handiwork should have remained just the same as when she climbed his knee and put it into his hand.

But it was not worthwhile to vex himself about a trifle. Midas now took his spectacles from his pocket and put them on his nose, in order that he might see more distinctly what he was about. In those days spectacles for common people had not been invented, but were already worn by kings; else, how could Midas have had any? To his great perplexity, however, excellent as the glasses were, he discovered that he could not possibly see through them. But this was the most natural thing in the world; for, on taking them off, the transparent crystals turned out to be plates of yellow metal, and, of course, were worthless as spectacles, though valuable as gold. It struck Midas as rather inconvenient, that, with all his wealth, he could never again be rich enough to own a pair of serviceable spectacles.

"It is no great matter, nevertheless," said he to himself very philosophically. "We cannot expect any great good without its being accompanied with some small inconvenience. The Golden Touch is worth the sacrifice of a pair of spectacles, at least, if not of one's very eyesight. My own eyes will serve for ordinary purposes, and little Marygold will soon be old enough to read to me."

Wise King Midas was so exalted by his good fortune that the palace seemed not sufficiently spacious to contain him. He therefore went downstairs, and smiled on observing that the balustrade of the staircase became a bar of burnished gold, as his hand passed over it in his descent. He lifted the door-latch (it was brass only a moment ago, but golden when his fingers quitted it) and emerged into the garden. Here, as it happened, he found a great number of beautiful roses in full bloom, and others in all the stages of lovely bud and blossom. Very delicious was their fragrance in the morning breeze. Their delicate blush was one of the fairest sights in the world; so gentle, so modest, and so full of sweet tranquility did these roses seem to be.

But Midas knew a way to make them far more precious, according to his way of thinking, than roses had ever been before. So he took great pains in going from bush to bush and exercised his magic touch most indefatigably, until every individual flower and bud, and even the worms at the heart of some of them, were changed to gold. By the time this good work was completed, King Midas was summoned to breakfast; and, as the morning air had given him an excellent appetite, he made haste back to the palace.

What was usually a king's breakfast in the days of Midas, I really do not know, and cannot stop now to investigate. To the best of my belief,

however, on this particular morning the breakfast consisted of hotcakes, some nice little brook trout, roasted potatoes, fresh boiled eggs, and coffee for King Midas himself, and a bowl of bread and milk for his daughter Marygold. At all events, this is a breakfast fit to set before a king; and, whether he had it or not, King Midas could not have had a better.

Little Marygold had not yet made her appearance. Her father ordered her to be called, and seating himself at table, awaited the child's coming in order to begin his own breakfast. To do Midas justice he really loved his daughter, and loved her so much more this morning on account of the good fortune that had befallen him. It was not a great while before he heard her coming along the passageway, crying bitterly. This circumstance surprised him because Marygold was one of the cheerfullest little people whom you would see in a summer's day, and hardly shed a thimbleful of tears in a twelvemonth. When Midas heard her sobs, he determined to put little Marygold into better spirits by an agreeable surprise; so, leaning across the table, he touched his daughter's bowl (which was a China one with pretty figures all around it) and transmuted it to gleaming gold.

Meanwhile, Marygold slowly and disconsolately opened the door and showed herself with her apron at her eyes, still sobbing as if her heart would break.

"How now, my little lady!" cried Midas. "Pray what is the matter with you this bright morning?"

Marygold, without taking the apron from her eyes, held out her hand, in which was one of the roses that Midas had so recently transmuted.

"Beautiful!" exclaimed her father. "And what is there in this magnificent, golden rose to make you cry?"

"Ah, dear father!" answered the child as well as her sobs would let her, "it is not beautiful, but the ugliest flower that ever grew! As soon as I was dressed I ran into the garden to gather some roses for you, because I know you like them, and like them better when gathered by your daughter. But, oh dear, dear me! What do you think has happened? Such a misfortune! All the beautiful roses that smelled so sweetly and had so many lovely blushes are blighted and spoilt! They are grown quite yellow, as you see this one, and have no longer any fragrance! What can have been the matter with them?"

"Poh, my dear little girl—pray don't cry about it!" said Midas, who was ashamed to confess that he himself had wrought the change that so greatly afflicted her. "Sit down and eat your bread and milk! You will find it easy enough to exchange a golden rose like that, which will last hundreds of years, for an ordinary one, which would wither in a day."

"I don't care for such roses as this!" cried Marygold, tossing it contemptuously away. "It has no smell, and the hard petals prick my nose!"

The child sat down to table, but was so occupied with her grief for the blighted roses that she did not even notice the wonderful transmutation of her China bowl. Perhaps this was all for the better; for Marygold was accustomed to take pleasure in looking at the queer figures and strange trees and houses that were painted on the circumference of the bowl; and these ornaments were now entirely lost in the yellow hue of the metal.

Midas, meanwhile, had poured out a cup of coffee; and, as a matter of course, the coffeepot, whatever metal it may have been when he took it up, was gold when he set it down. He thought to himself that it was rather an extravagant style of splendor, in a king of his simple habits, to breakfast off a service of gold, and he began to be puzzled with the difficulty of keeping his treasures safe. The cupboard and the kitchen would no longer be a secure place of deposit for articles so valuable as golden bowls and coffeepots.

Amid these thoughts he lifted a spoonful of coffee to his lips, and sipping it, was astonished to perceive that the instant his lips touched the liquid it became molten gold, and the next moment, hardened into a lump!

"Ha!" exclaimed Midas, rather aghast.

"What is the matter, father?" asked little Marygold, gazing at him with the tears still standing in her eyes.

"Nothing, child, nothing!" said Midas. "Eat your milk before it gets quite cold."

He took one of the nice little trouts on his plate and, by way of experiment, touched its tail with his finger. To his horror it was immediately transmuted from an admirably fried brook trout into a gold fish, though not one of those goldfishes that people often keep in glass globes, as ornaments for the parlor. No, but it was really a metallic fish, and looked as if it had been very cunningly made by the nicest goldsmith in the world. Its little bones were now golden wires; its fins and tail were thin plates of gold; and there were marks of the fork in it, and all the delicate, frothy appearance of a nicely fried fish, exactly imitated in metal. A very pretty piece of work, as you may suppose; only King Midas, just at that moment, would much rather have had a real trout in his dish than this elaborate and valuable imitation of one.

"I don't quite see," thought he to himself, "how I am to get any breakfast!"

He took one of the smoking hotcakes and had scarcely broken it when, to his cruel mortification, though a moment before it had been the whitest wheat, it assumed the yellow hue of Indian meal. To say the truth, if it had really been a hot Indian cake, Midas would have prized it a good deal more than he now did, when its solidity and increased weight made him too bitterly sensible that it was gold. Almost in despair, he helped himself to a boiled egg, which immediately underwent a change similar to those of the trout and the cake. The egg, indeed, might have been mistaken for one of those that the famous goose in the storybook was in the habit of laying; but King Midas was the only goose that had had anything to do with the matter.

"Well, this is a quandary!" thought he, leaning back in his chair and looking quite enviously at little Marygold, who was now eating her bread and milk with great satisfaction. "Such a costly breakfast before me, and nothing that can be eaten!"

Hoping that by dint of great dispatch he might avoid what he now felt to be a considerable inconvenience, King Midas next snatched a hot potato and attempted to cram it into his mouth and swallow it in a hurry. But the Golden Touch was too nimble for him. He found his mouth full, not of mealy potato, but of solid metal, which so burnt his tongue that he roared aloud, and, jumping up from the table, he began to dance and stamp about the room, both with pain and affright.

"Father, dear father!" cried little Marygold, who was a very affectionate child, "pray what is the matter? Have you burnt your mouth?"

"Ah, dear child," groaned Midas dolefully, "I don't know what is to become of your poor father!"

And truly, my dear little folks, did you ever hear of such a pitiable case in all your lives? Here was literally the richest breakfast that could be set before a king, and its very richness made it absolutely good for nothing. The poorest laborer, sitting down to his crust of bread and cup of water, was far better off than King Midas, whose delicate food was really worth its weight in gold. And what was to be done? Already, at breakfast, Midas was excessively hungry. Would he be less so by dinnertime? And how ravenous would be his appetite for supper, which must undoubtedly consist of the same sort indigestible dishes as those now before him! How many days, think you, would he survive a continuance of this rich fare? These reflections so troubled wise King Midas that he began to doubt whether, after all, riches are the one desirable thing in the world, or even the most desirable. But this was only a passing thought. So fascinated was Midas with the glitter of the yellow metal that he would still have refused to give up the Golden Touch for so paltry a consideration as breakfast. Just imagine what a price for one meal's victuals! It would have been the same as paying millions and millions of money (and as many millions more as would take forever to reckon up) for some fried trout, an egg, a potato, a hotcake, and a cup of coffee!

"It would be quite too dear," thought Midas.

Nevertheless, so great was his hunger, and the perplexity of his situation, that he again groaned aloud, and very greviously too. Our pretty Marygold could endure it no longer. She sat a moment, gazing at her father and trying with all the might of her little wits to find out what was the matter with him. Then, with a sweet and sorrowful impulse to comfort him, she started from her chair and, running to Midas, threw her arms affectionately about his knees. He bent down and kissed her. He felt that his little daughter's love was worth a thousand times more than he had gained by the Golden Touch.

"My precious, precious Marygold!" cried he.

But Marygold made no answer.

Alas, what had he done? How fatal was the gift that the stranger bestowed! The moment the lips of Midas touched Marygold's forehead a change had taken place. Her sweet rosy face, so full of affection as it had been, assumed a glittering yellow color, with yeallow teardrops congealing on her cheeks. Her beautiful, brown ringlets took the same tint. Her soft and tender little form grew hard and inflexible within her father's encircling arms. O terrible misfortune! The victim of his insatiable desire for wealth, little Marygold was a human child no longer, but a golden statue!

Yes, there she was, with the questioning look of love, grief, and pity hardened into her face. It was the prettiest and most woeful sight that ever mortal saw. All the features and tokens of Marygold were there; even the beloved little dimple remained in her golden chin. But, the more perfect was the resemblance, the greater was the father's agony at beholding this golden image, which was all that was left him of a daughter. It had been a favorite phrase of Midas, whenever he felt particularly fond of the child, to say that she was worth her weight in gold. And now the phrase had become literally true. And now, at last, when it was too late, he felt how infinitely a warm and tender heart that loved him exceeded in value all the wealth that could be piled up betwixt the earth and sky!

It would be too sad a story if I were to tell you how Midas, in the fullness of all his gratified desires, began to wring his hands and bemoan himself; and how he could neither bear to look at Marygold, nor yet to look away from her. Except when his eyes were fixed on the image, he could not possibly believe that she was changed to gold. But stealing another glance, there was the precious little figure, with a yellow teardrop on its yellow cheek, and a look so piteous and tender that it seemed as if that very

expression must needs soften the gold and make it flesh again. This, however, could not be. So Midas had only to wring his hands and to wish that he were the poorest man in the wide world if the loss of all his wealth might bring back the faintest rose-color to his dear child's face.

While he was in this tumult of despair he suddenly beheld a stranger standing near the door. Midas bent down his head without speaking; for he recognized the same figure that had appeared to him the day before in the treasure-room, and had bestowed on him this disastrous faculty of the Golden Touch. The stranger's countenance still wore a smile, which seemed to shed a yellow luster all about the room, and gleamed on little Marygold's image, and on the other objects that had been transmuted by the touch of Midas.

"Well, friend Midas," said the stranger, "pray how do you succeed with the Golden Touch?"

Midas shook his head. "I am very miserable," said he.

"Very miserable, indeed!" exclaimed the stranger. "And how happens that? Have I not faithfully kept my promise with you? Have you not everything that your heart desired?"

"Gold is not everything," answered Midas. "And I have lost all that my heart really cared for."

"Ah! So you have made a discovery since yesterday?" observed the stranger. "Let us see then. Which of these two things do you think is really worth the most—the gift of the Golden Touch, or one cup of clear, cold water?"

"O blessed water!" exclaimed Midas. "It will never moisten my parched throat again!"

"The Golden Touch," continued the stranger, "or a crust of bread?"

"A piece of bread," answered Midas, "is worth all the gold on earth!"

"The Golden Touch," asked the stranger, "or your own little Marygold warm, soft, and loving, as she was an hour ago?"

"O my child, my dear child!" cried poor Midas ringing his hands. "I would not have given that one small dimple in her chin for the power of changing this whole big earth into a solid lump of gold!"

"You are wiser than you were, King Midas!" said the stranger, looking seriously at him. "Your own heart, I perceive, has not been entirely changed from flesh to gold. Were it so, your case would indeed be desperate. But you appear to be still capable of understanding that the commonest things, such as lie within everybody's grasp, are more valuable than the riches that so many mortals sigh and struggle after. Tell me, now, do you sincerely desire to rid yourself of this Golden Touch?"

"It is hateful to me!" replied Midas.

A fly settled on his nose, but immediately fell to the floor; for it, too, had become gold. Midas shuddered.

"Go, then," said the stranger, "and plunge into the river that glides past the bottom of your garden. Take likewise a vase of the same water, and sprinkle it over any object that you may desire to change back again from gold into its former substance. If you do this in earnestness and sincerity, it may possibly repair the mischief that your avarice has occasioned."

King Midas bowed low; and when he lifted his head, the lustrous stranger had vanished.

You will easily believe that Midas lost no time in snatching up a great earthen pitcher (but, alas me! it was no longer earthen after he touched it) and hastening to the riverside. As he scampered along and forced his way

through the shrubbery, it was positively marvelous to see how the foliage turned yellow behind him, as if the autumn had been there, and nowhere else. On reaching the river's bank, he plunged headlong in, without waiting so much as to pull off his shoes.

"Uoof! Poof! Poof!" snorted King Midas as his head emerged out of the water. "Well; this is really a refreshing bath, and I think it must have quite washed away the Golden Touch. And now for filling my pitcher!"

As he dipped the pitcher into the water it gladdened his very heart to see it change from gold into the same good, honest earthen vessel that had been before he touched it. He was conscious also of a change within himself. A cold, hard, and heavy weight seemed to have gone out of his bosom. No doubt his heart had been gradually losing its human substance and transmuting itself into insensible metal, but had now softened back again into flesh. Perceiving a violet that grew on the bank of the river, Midas touched it with his finger and was overjoyed to find that the delicate flower retained its purple hue instead of undergoing a yellow blight. The curse of the Golden Touch had, therefore, really been removed from him.

King Midas hastened back to the palace; and, I suppose, the servants knew not what to make of it when they saw their royal master so carefully bringing home an earthen pitcher of water. But that water, which was to undo all the mischief that his folly had wrought, was more precious to Midas than an ocean of molten gold could have been. The first thing he did, as you need hardly be told, was to sprinkle it by handfuls over the golden figure of little Marygold.

No sooner did it fall on her than you would have laughed to see how the rosy color came back to the dear child's cheek!—and how she began to sneeze and sputter!—and how astonished she was to find herself dripping wet, and her father still throwing more water over her!

"Pray do not, dear father!" cried she. "See how you have wet my nice frock, which I put on only this morning!"

For Marygold did not know that she had been a little golden statue; nor could she remember anything that had happened since the moment when she ran with outstretched arms to comfort poor King Midas.

Her father did not think it necessary to tell his beloved child how very foolish he had been, but contented himself with showing how much wiser he had now grown. For this purpose, he led little Marygold into the garden, where he sprinkled all the remainder of the water over the rosebushes, and with such good effect that above five thousand roses recovered their beautiful bloom. There were two circumstances, however, that as long as he lived used to put King Midas in mind of the Golden Touch. One was that the sands of the river sparkled like gold; the other, that little Marygold's hair had now a golden tinge, which he had never observed in it before she had been transmuted by the effect of his kiss. This change of hue was really an improvement, and made Marygold's hair richer than in her babyhood.

When King Midas had grown quite an old man, and used to trot Marygold's children on his knee, he was fond of telling them this marvelous story, pretty much as I have now told it to you. And then would he stroke their glossy ringlets and tell them that their hair, likewise, had a rich shade of gold, which they had inherited from their mother.

"And, to tell you the truth, my precious little folks," quoth King Midas, diligently trotting the children all the while, "ever since that morning, I have hated the very sight of all other gold, save this!"